T0088727

Doreen Smith

Cello Sight-Reading

Book 2

NOTE

These graded sight-reading pieces for the cello are designed to provide practice material at all stages. Book 1 begins with the first position and covers the usual examination expectations for the earlier grades. More advanced players will find exercises requiring use of the higher registers, tenor and treble clefs, and the need for more technical expertise in book 2.

Fingering and bowing

There are as many fingerings and bowings as there are players. Those marked here are simply one way of performing a piece; they are by no means obligatory. The aim is to give as musical an impression as possible after a brief study of the piece, and to enjoy exploring the instrument.

To the cellist — what to do before you play

Look at:

- The **foreign words** which will suggest the speed, mood, and style.
- The **key signature**: work out your finger patterns on each string.
- The **time signature**: are you going to count in beats, or would it be more helpful to subdivide each beat?
- **Changes** of clef, key signature, or time signature (in higher grades).
- **Unusual** time patterns, accidentals, rests, staccato notes, slurs, and dynamics.
- The **speed**: decide on the speed and count at least one bar before you begin. Count aloud throughout.

Keep going, and try to give an overall impression of the music.

Doreen Smith, 1992

CELLO SIGHT-READING, BOOK 2

by DOREEN SMITH

GRADE 6

© Oxford University Press 1978 and 1992

OXFORD UNIVERSITY PRESS, MUSIC DEPARTMENT, WALTON STREET, OXFORD OX2 6DP

Photocopying this copyright material is ILLEGAL.

Lamentoso
5
p
mp
cresc.
Vivace
6
mf
cresc.
Moderato
7
mf
f
Allegretto grazioso
8
mp
p
dim.

Adagio
9
mf cantabile
p
mf
dim.
Allegro
10
mf
mp
cresc.
pizz.
f
Andante espressivo
11
mp
Andantino grazioso
12
p
mf
poco rit.

Alla mazurka
13
mp
cresc.
leggiero
Vivo
14
mf
p
pizz.
arco
cresc.
Pastorale
15
mf
II
cresc.
Comodo
16
mp
cresc.

Moderato
17
mp
cresc.
Affettuoso
18
mp
Piacevole
19
mp
p
poco rall.
a tempo
p
Dolente
20
mp molto legato
cresc.
dim. e rit.

GRADE 7

Comodo
1
mp
cresc.
mf
pizz.
Alla gavotta
2
mp
pizz.
Lento
3
p cantabile
mp
mf
cresc.
dim.
Allegretto
4
mp cantabile
dolce
pizz.

Moderato
5
mp
II
II
Andante
6
mf
p
dim.
pizz.
Alla marcia
7
mf
p

Largo
8
mp cantabile
Allegro vivace
9
mf
rit.
Vivace
10
f
mp
cresc.
Lento
11
p
cresc.
dim.
pizz.
arco
p

Piacevole
12
mf
rit.
ad lib.
rit.
a tempo
tr
Allegretto
13
f
rit.
a tempo
scherzando
p
cresc.
poco rall.
Allegro moderato
14
mf
meno f
cresc.

Andante espressivo
15
p
Vivo
16
f scherzando
meno mosso
dolce
poco rit.
a tempo
mp scherzando
cresc.
Poco vivo
17
mp
meno mosso
espressivo
poco vivo

Moderato
18
mf
poco meno mosso
p
poco rall.
Tempo primo
p
cresc. e poco rall.
Andante
19
mf marcato
p
cresc.
non legato
p
Allegretto dolce
20
mp
pizz.
arco
mp
pizz.

GRADE 8

Alla giga
1
mf
mp
cresc.
pizz.
Allegretto
2
mp
II
cresc.
cresc.
cresc.
f
Con brio
3
f
mp
p
cresc.

Allegretto
4
mp legato
cantabile
Larghetto
5
mp
mf
Presto
6
f
pizz.
arco
cresc.
pizz.

Allegro
7
mf
cresc.
cresc.
Lento
8
II
mp
II
cresc.
II
dim. e rit.
Allegretto
9
mf
mp
p
Scherzando
10
mf
dim.
f

Andante
11
p
poco cresc.
poco rit.
rall.
tempo rubato
rall.
a tempo
p
cresc.
Comodo
12
mf
doppio movimento
non legato
rit.
a tempo
mp
cresc.

Adagio
13
mf
cresc.
cresc.
Alla gavotta
14
mp
mp
cresc.
p

Allegretto
15
mf
p
cresc.
rit.
Lento assai
16
mf
dim. e poco rit.
a tempo
mf

Allegro moderato
17
mf
p
Piacevole
18
p
mf
poco rit.
a tempo
p
cresc.
p
poco cresc.

Vivace
19
f
Meno mosso
mp
rit. e dim.
tempo primo
mf
pizz.
Allegretto teneramente
20
mp
pizz.
arco
mf
più f